# *Where the IT Lifecycle Ends*

How non-compliant IT Asset Disposition
creates unnecessary exposure.

Kyle A. Marks

ISBN: 9798882570339


Cover design:   Kyle A. Marks
Illustrations:    Billy Chrisnada
Library of Congress Control Number: 2018675309
Printed in the United States of America

# Introduction

The non-compliant IT asset disposition (ITAD) issue is an unspeakable problem that came to light recently when a major bank disclosed two data breaches. The Office of the Comptroller of the Currency (OCC) imposed a $60 million penalty on the bank for engaging in "unsound practices that were part of a pattern of misconduct." The Securities and Exchange Commission (SEC) fined another $35 million, describing the bank's ITAD procedures as "astonishing."

While the word "astonishing" captures the severity of the issue, I worry about the word choice. Finding a stronger adjective may be challenging once the widespread nature of the problem is fully recognized.

The SEC has implemented new cybersecurity regulations and started holding executives personally accountable for ignoring vulnerabilities. I believe cartoons can make non-compliant ITAD more understandable and accessible. This book aims to shed light on the problem and offer a solution.

Good luck on your journey!

Kyle Marks

The IT lifecycle begins when an asset is acquired and ends when it is decommissioned and retired. While compliance mandates meticulous tracking of every asset from acquisition to disposition, it is commonly known that most organizations can't account for up to 20% of hardware assets.

Organizations can no longer kick the can down the road. The SEC passed cybersecurity regulations and deemed IT asset disposition (ITAD) a cybersecurity risk after discovering routine procedures were "astonishing."

The traditional IT asset management (ITAM)-ITAD paradigm has its roots in trust. The same people are responsible for both tracking assets and retiring them. Organizations can no longer afford to let the fox guard the henhouse. Segregation of duties (SOD) is essential to avoid conflicts of interest and satisfy regulatory requirements.

Despite its noble goals, traditional ITAD is destined to fail since it lacks SOD. While ITAM experts often downplay the need for SOD, implementing it would ironically enhance accountability and significantly benefit ITAM by increasing its resources.

ITAM and ITAD vendors support one another and have each other's backs. Traditional, trust-based ITAD is rigged to skirt accountability and disclosure provisions.

Rather than being investigated, missing IT assets are considered retired. Retired assets are assigned to ITAD vendors. Allocating assets transfers the burden of inventory reconciliation to the ITAD vendor, who has no incentive to report issues.

IT assets turn toxic when they go missing without proof that they don't contain data. Management may be reluctant to examine non-compliant ITAD because they fear it may open a Pandora's Box of complex and costly challenges with toxic IT assets.

Loss aversion explains why ITAM and ITAD vendors are reluctant to report assets missing. People naturally avoid self-reporting facts that could make them look bad.

Problems with traditional, trust-based, non-compliant ITAD are beyond the control of any one individual.

Marks

Blaming individuals for non-compliant ITAD practices creates a culture of fear, which hinders problem-solving and increases whistleblower risk.

The elephant in the room is an inherent conflict of interest. Dealing with conflicts of interest can be risky and unpleasant without an effective strategy. Anyone can submit a whistleblower tip to the SEC.

Marks

While relying on ITAM might be tempting, conflicts of interest compromise it as the issues stem from there. Given the potential consequences, seeking assistance from an ITAD management specialist is prudent.

While ITAM can't resolve non-compliant ITAD, effective ITAM remains vital to preventing future issues. Assets must be tracked from acquisition through disposition, and assets can go missing at any stage of the lifecycle.

Effective ITAM requires the right incentive structure, appropriate resources, and executive support. When incentives aren't aligned, incidents go unreported.

In traditional, trust-based ITAD, it's easy to sweep problems under the rug, making issues tempting for management to overlook.

Exposure has escalated as both the SEC and ambulance chasers have uncovered the issue of non-compliant ITAD.

The SEC now holds management accountable for being aware of incidents. Boards have new responsibilities, and plausible deniability is not a justifiable excuse.

Cyber liability insurance will not protect an organization from non-compliant ITAD. Hidden in the fine print are terms and conditions you must comply with, including adequate controls and SOD.

Independent auditors will scrutinize processes because the SEC rules spotlight ITAD, demanding robust inventory tracking and internal controls. Any discrepancy between the company's and the ITAD vendor's inventory will require a thorough investigation.

It may seem like being painted into a corner because the past can't be changed, those responsible must remain involved, and anyone can become a whistleblower. Change is required for compliance. However, mismanaging the shift may create additional exposure.

The myriad challenges tied to toxic IT assets and non-compliant ITAD can be overwhelming. Transforming ITAM-ITAD requires embracing change and engaging a specialist.

Disposal tags are crucial for managing assets, preventing theft, minimizing losses, and ensuring a clear chain of custody. They bring order and discipline to the disposal process.

A policy of using disposal tags can instantly transform ITAD and set the foundation for defensible disposition. Disposal tags discreetly address issues, deter theft, and prove the chain of custody. Disposal tags are like a vet hiding medicine in treats.

Just as skydivers wouldn't dream of jumping without a backup parachute, an equipment verification hold (EVH) when an ITAD vendor receives the assets acts as a critical safety net in the ITAD process. This temporary halt ensures equipment isn't resold or destroyed until its chain of custody is verified.

The SEC incentivizes whistleblower tips with millions of dollars. Where the IT lifecycle ends, there may be regulatory fines and lawsuits if adequate controls are not in place, such as segregation of duties, disposal tags, and equipment verification holds.

By implementing segregation of duties, disposal tags, and equipment verification holds, your organization can safeguard against non-compliant ITAD. With these controls in place, there is peace of mind and compliance where the IT lifecycle ends.

# Afterword

ITAD has become a compliance nightmare and a plaintiff lawyer's dream. Cartoons can simplify complex topics and spark open dialogue, making difficult conversations more manageable.

Here are a few questions to ask to get the conversations started:

- How would you know if an employee took an asset?
- How would you know if a truck driver stole an asset?
- How would you know if a missing asset is retired rather than being investigated?
- What incentives exist to report a security incident?
- Does your organization consider a missing asset a cybersecurity incident?
- Do you share your inventory with your ITAD vendor?
- Do you require your ITAD vendor to hold assets to confirm the chain of custody?
- Is the individual responsible for tracking assets also in charge of disposal?

For further information, please feel free to contact or follow me. You can also find valuable insights in my blog, The ITAD Aficionado.

# About The Author

## Kyle A. Marks

Kyle is an ITAD enthusiast and CEO of Retire-IT, an independent consulting firm specializing in IT Asset Disposition management. Over the past 20 years, Kyle has managed more than 20,000 ITAD projects. Kyle served Arrow Electronics as the President of US Micro. Ages ago, Kyle was a consultant with Bain & Company and in marketing with Maybelline L'Oréal. Kyle has an economics degree from Rhodes College, an MBA from Harvard Business School, and is the proud father of two wonderfully inexhaustible kids.

Kyle can be reached at:
www.Retire-IT.com/itad-aficionado
www.linkedin.com/in/kylemarks
www.twitter.com/RetireIT